MUSHROOM RAIN

Laura K. Zimmermann

Illustrated by Jamie Green

Published by Sleeping Bear Press™

Without warning,
they appear.

Mushrooms!

Delicate **umbrellas** open,

red octopus arms rise from the ground,

cupped nests with eggs appear.

In darkness, a spooky green
glows under a starlit sky.

Bizarre blooms with strange scents—
some like bubble gum, coconut, maple syrup . . .
others, the stench of burnt hair, rotten cabbage, or animals long dead.

Many are tattered and torn
by hungry visitors

chomping,

scraping,

gnawing,

and **burrowing.**

Some mushrooms are harvested and stored.

Red squirrels dry them in branches,
ants pile foraged pieces in their nests,
while mushroom hunters, baskets in hand, stalk silent prey.

Then, without warning,
mushrooms disappear,

no longer seen, but not gone.

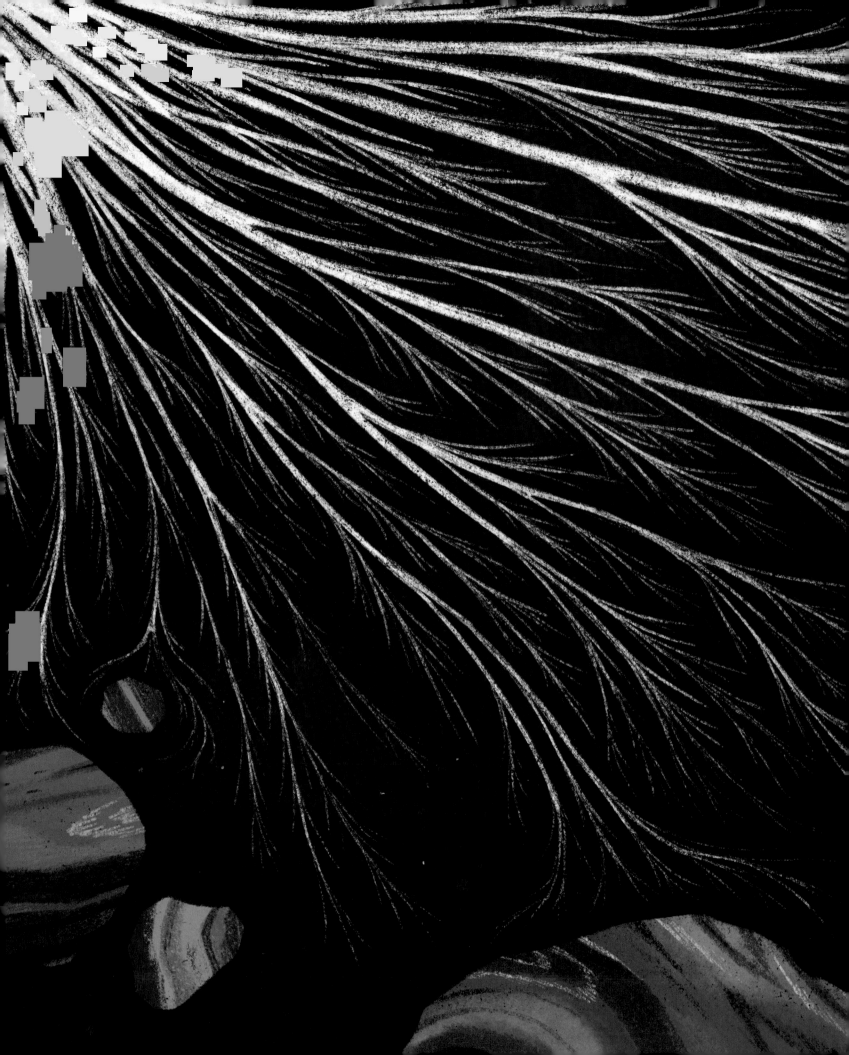

For **beneath** a mushroom's bloom,
a hidden form reaches out,
sheltered and secretly wandering

The largest has sprawled under a forest for **thousands** of years.

It stretches for miles—
still wandering.

It continues to grow.

Blooms cast new mushrooms even farther

when scattered spores,

like a flower's **seeds**,

settle on the forest **floor.**

Tiny threads too small to see
branch out,
growing bigger . . .

they pack together
and rise.

But not all spores land in the forest.

Some—
    caught by the **wind**—

soar to the **sky**,
    seeding **clouds**.

They help create **rain**.

Droplets fall,
   strange blooms spring up,

after a *mushroom rain.*

MORE to KNOW ABOUT MUSHROOMS!

Mushroom rain is a translation of a Russian phrase **gribnoy dozhd'** (greeb-noy DOH-zsht) that means a light rain while the sun is shining—it's thought to be good growing weather for mushrooms.

Mushrooms come in a rainbow of colors and shapes, with smells from delightful to disgusting. They can be rough and ragged, smooth, felted, waxy, slimy, or even a melting ooze.

With their "blooms" above and threads spreading below, you might think mushroom-producing fungi are a kind of plant. But they aren't. In fact, they are more closely related to animals like you! Unlike plants, fungi can't make their own food through photosynthesis. They have to find food like animals. But unlike animals, fungi digest outside of their body instead of within, so they are different from animals, too.

GILLS: the papery ribs that hang down from a mushroom cap. Gills create and release spores for mushrooms, but only for those that have gills. Mushroom caps without gills have tiny holes or small icicle-like spikes.

SPORES: create new mushroom-producing fungi, much as seeds do for plants.

FRUITING BODY: the part of mushroom-producing fungi we usually see (the "mushroom" or "bloom"). It produces spores and comes in different shapes—many, but not all, have a cap and a stalk. When mushrooms appear, it's called a fruiting.

GERMINATION: occurs when the spore of a mushroom or the seed of a plant begins to grow.

MYCELIUM (my-see-lee-um): a weblike collection of hyphae. It is hidden under the mushrooms we see.

HYPHAE (high-fee): tiny hairlike tubes that form a mycelium. They are how a mushroom "eats." The hyphae of decomposer mushrooms use enzymes to break down (decompose) dead and decaying matter to get the nutrients they need, much like your stomach does with the food you eat.

OUT OF SIGHT

When a spore begins to grow, it sends out tiny hyphae—they are so tiny, you need a microscope to see them. The hyphae branch out to form a network called a mycelium. For mushrooms that grow on the ground, the mycelium spreads under the soil. When conditions are right, portions of the mycelium pack together, creating mushrooms that rise up as the bizarre "blooms" we see.

WHERE DO MUSHROOMS LIVE?

Many mushroom spores germinate on the forest floor, but not all do. Some germinate in other places, like beneath the bark of trees, on fallen branches and stumps, or in dung. Others grow outside of the forest in lawns, meadows, mountains, salt marshes, and even sand dunes.

HUMONGOUS FUNGUS

The biggest mushroom-producing fungus in the world grows in the Blue Mountains of Eastern Oregon. It is the largest known living organism on Earth. Its mushrooms (fruiting bodies) and mycelium combined are thought to weigh more than 50 blue whales. Scientists guess it is thousands of years old!

WHO LIKES to EAT MUSHROOMS?

Many animals eat mushrooms. Some chomp, nibble, or gnaw, with large or small bites. Land snails and slugs scrape the mushroom using thousands of tiny teeth. Insect larvae are wormlike younger versions of insects. Larvae that feed on mushrooms burrow into them, creating tunnels as they munch and move through the mushroom.

Mushroom-harvesting ants, **Euprenolepis procera**, are a kind of ant that brings pieces of mushroom back to their nest. There they put them in a pile until they turn to mush. Mushy mushrooms are the main thing these ants eat.

Red squirrels gather mushrooms and hang them in trees or place them on logs and stumps to dry before storing them.

Human mushroom hunters love finding tasty mushrooms. But they have to be careful. Some mushrooms are good to eat, but others are poisonous. Never pick or eat a wild mushroom unless an expert says it's safe.

EUPRENOLEPIS PROCERA EATING PLEUROTUS DJAMOR

SEEDING the CLOUDS

Millions of tons of mushroom spores soar to the sky each year. Like plants, clouds grow from seeds. But unlike plant seeds, which grow from life inside, cloud seeds collect water on the outside. Mushroom spores are one kind of cloud seed. In the atmosphere, water vapor clings to spores creating small droplets of water or ice. A cloud is made up of billions and trillions of droplets made from spores and other small cloud seed particles, like dust. Within the cloud, they clump together, making bigger and bigger droplets. Once the droplets are heavy enough, they fall as rain, soaking the forest so new mushrooms can grow.

FUN with MUSHROOMS

MAKE SPORE PRINTS

To make a spore print of a mushroom with gills, you first need a mushroom. Get the freshest you can find at a store or farmers market. Never pick one from outdoors unless a mushroom expert tells you it is safe—some wild mushrooms can make you really sick.

- Cut off the stem so you can see the gills.
- Turn the mushroom over so the gills are facing down, and put it on a light-colored piece of paper.
- Put a drop of water on top to help the spores come out.
- Cover with a cup and leave it someplace safe overnight.
- Carefully lift the mushroom and see what the spores left behind!

NOTICE and WONDER

Study the pictures in the book. What kinds of animals, plants, and mushrooms do you see? How are the mushrooms different and how are they the same?

Go on a walk and notice the mushrooms around you. What colors, shapes, and sizes do you see? Does it look like animals have been there? Imagine tiny threads spreading beneath the mushroom blooms. How far do you think they go? If you don't see any mushrooms, why do you think that is?

Do some research and see what you find. Start with these questions and see where they lead you. What do mushroom-producing fungi need to survive? Did you know they help trees communicate? How do they do this? What else do you want to know about mushrooms?

WANT TO LEARN EVEN MORE ABOUT MUSHROOMS?

Further Reading

Gravel, Elise. *The Mushroom Fan Club*. Montreal: Enfant, 2018.

Keller, Joy. *Fungus is Among Us!* Seattle: Innovation Press, 2019.

Watkins II, Te'Lario. *Te'Lario's Amazing Mushroom Farm*. Rochester: West Publishing Group, 2017.

Selected Bibliography

Hassett, Maribeth O., Mark W. F. Fischer, and Nicholas P. Money. "Mushrooms as Rainmakers: How Spores Act as Nuclei for Raindrops." *PLOS One* 10, no. 10 (2015): e0140407.

Marley, Greg A. *Chanterelle Dreams, Amanita Nightmares: The Love, Lore, and Mystique of Mushrooms*. Vermont: Chelsea Green Publishing, 2010.

Oregon Field Guide. "Humongous Fungus." PBS video, 7:26. February 12, 2015. https://www.pbs.org/video/oregon-field-guide-humongous-fungus/.

Sheldrake, Merlin. *Entangled Life: How Fungi Make Our Worlds, Change Our Minds & Shape Our Futures*. New York: Random House, 2020.

Woo, Cheolwoon, Choa An, Siyu Xu, Seuhg-Muk Yi, and Naomichi Yamamoto. "Taxonomic Diversity of Fungi Deposited from the Atmosphere." *The ISME Journal* 12, no. 8, 2051–2060 (2018). https://doi.org/10.1038/s41396-018-0160-7.

To my family and friends,
who believed when I did not
—Laura

To mushrooms and C. C.—
both for keeping me curious
—Jamie

Laura K. Zimmermann and Sleeping Bear Press wish to thank the
following individuals for their insightful feedback and guidance:
Nik Money, mycologist and science writer; Lee Whitford;
Darvin DeShazer; Scott Camazine; Bill Sheehan, PhD, President,
Fungal Diversity Survey; Dr. Kristen Wickert; and
Dr. Albert Torzilli, emeritus professor,
George Mason University.

SLEEPING BEAR PRESS™

10 9 8 7 6 5 4

Library of Congress Cataloging-in-Publication Data | Names: Zimmermann, Laura K., author. | Green, Jamie (Illustrator), illustrator. | Title: Mushroom rain / by Laura K. Zimmermann ; illustrated
by Jamie Green. | Description: Ann Arbor : Sleeping Bear Press, [2022] | Audience: Ages 4–8. | Summary: "Through lyrical text and colorful detailed artwork, the mysterious and sometimes bizarre
world of mushrooms is explored. Back matter includes a glossary and science facts"– Provided by publisher. | Identifiers: LCCN 2021037583 | ISBN 9781534111509 (hardcover)
Subjects: LCSH: Mushrooms—Juvenile literature. | CYAC: Mushrooms. | Classification: LCC QK617 .Z55 2022 | DDC 579.6–dc23 | LC record available at https://lccn.loc.gov/2021037583